# ABC's

to

FOCUS

By

LaToya Crawford

Published by
Get It "Write" Consulting, LLC
Valdosta, GA 31602

ISBN 978-0-9915764-4-9

Some messages were inspired by Joel Osteen Ministries

www.getitwrite-consulting.com

# *Dedication*

## To Andre

I didn't think that God would ever bless me with you. I didn't think that I was capable of having you. BUT you arrived September 7, 2007 and my life has never been the same.

I love you, Andre Williams, Jr.—my only child. I dedicate my first book to you!

## *Inspirational Moment*

### I did it! I finished the book!

I have been writing *The ABC's to Focus* for nearly two years. I would work on a letter every now and then. Unfortunately, I got distracted and could never finish the book. Thankfully, I would watch Joel Osteen every Sunday evening, and his sermons would inspire me to get back to my dreams. In fact, seeing him in person pushed me to get back to the pages. I had the incredible opportunity to see him in Tallahassee, Florida in 2014 during "A Night of Hope." His ministries sent me two, great bottom section tickets to the event.

Letters U, V, X, and Y, might sound familiar. They were inspired by Joel Osteen Ministries.

# *Introduction*

## F.O.C.U.S
"Your Gifts Will Make Room For You If You FOCUS."

**F**orget About the Past

**O**verlook Negative Thoughts and People

**C**oncentrate on the Task

**U**nderstand that there is a Bigger Picture

**S**peak Life into Every Situation

# Activation Brings Speculation

Once your purpose is activated in you, the devil **sets** out to stop you. You are now a target for the enemy because the adversary understands that you are a threat to the kingdom of Hell. Activation of your purpose pushes the enemy to bring forth fear, rejection, doubt, and confusion. When you activate your purpose, get ready to fight for your destiny.

*2 Timothy 1:6*
"Wherefore I put thee in remembrance that thou stir up the gift of God, which is in thee by the putting on my hands. 7. For God hath not given us the spirit of fear; but of power, love, and of a sound mind. 8. Be not thou therefore ashamed of the testimony of our Lord, nor of me his prisoner: but be thou partaker of the afflictions of the gospel according to the power of God."

# Broken But Blessed

Even though you might be broken, you are still blessed. You might be in despair but you still have destiny. You might even feel frustrated but God still holds your future. I am reminded of the Last Supper when Jesus before his disciples took the bread, blessed it, and then broke it. So, you were blessed even before the breaking. The blessing before the break proves that you were already anointed before the pain. You must be broken every now and then so you don't forget about Jesus…He goes to tell his disciples to "do it in remembrance of me." If we don't ever suffer we might forget about the Savior. If we are constantly in our palace, we might forget about the pit. We are victorious even in the valley so let's shout now before reaching the mountaintop!

*Matthew 26: 26*

"And as they were eating, Jesus took bread, and blessed it, and brake it, and gave it to the disciples, and said, Take, eat, this is my body."

Psalm 20: 7 "Some trust in chariots, and some in horses: but we will REMEMBER the name of the Lord our God."

# Consistent Christians Are Considered

The reason why you are constantly tested is because you are a consistent Christian. You always find yourself praying, praising, and trying to please God. God is not looking for situational saints, but he longs for those people that will follow him no matter what the circumstance looks like. Count it an honor to be considered because although you might be on the losing team now, God is going to give you double for your trouble. My mind goes back to Job. He lost everything but he refused to charge God. Since Job was a consistent Christian, he was considered.

*Job 1: 8*

"And the Lord said unto Satan, Hast thou CONSIDERED my servant Job, that there is none like him in the earth, a perfect and upright man, one that feareth God, and escheweth evil?"

*Job 42: 10*

"And the Lord turned the captivity of Job, when he prayed for his friends: also the Lord gave Job twice as much as he had before."

# Dismiss Distractions

In order to reach your goals, you have to stay focused. The devil is designed to kill, steal, destroy, and distract you from achieving your dreams! Please understand that a distraction is not procrastination. You become distracted when you have already set out to accomplish your purpose, but procrastination is the process of not moving forward at all. You must Dismiss anything or anybody that takes your eyes off the prize. Be mindful of your time, friends, assignments, and destinations. If they don't help deliver your destiny, then they are distracting your destiny.

*I Peter 5:8*

"Be sober, be vigilant; because your adversary the devil, as a roaring lion, walketh about, seeking whom he may devour."

*Philippians 3:13-14*
"...forgetting those things which are behind, and reaching forth unto those things which are before.  14. I press toward the mark for the prize of the high calling of God in Christ Jesus."

# Enemies Equal Elevation

When you begin to recognize and realize that you have more enemies than friends, don't get upset; get excited. The bible reminds us that God will make your enemies your footstool. A footstool was created to raise the foot higher. Therefore, the more enemies you have the higher God is going to take you. It really is lonely at the top. So, if you find yourself climbing higher on the success ladder but more people are at the bottom of it trying to knock you down just know it is the will of GOD!

*Luke 20: 42-43*
"And David himself saith in the book of Psalms, The Lord said unto my Lord, Sit thou on my right hand, 43. Till I make thine Enemies thy footstool."

# Free Yourself

Many times people try to go higher in life but are carrying a heavy load. Scientifically, a plane that is oversized can't get off the ground. The bible reminds us in Hebrews to lay aside every weight and in Romans we are commanded to let nothing separate us from the love of God. Sometimes we have to cut ties with some special people and some habits. Your weight might be a job, relationships, or even a mindset. You will never reach your maximum altitude with too much baggage weighing you down. As hard as it is sometimes, we have to let go of some stuff and some people.

*Hebrews 12:1*
"Wherefore seeing we also are compassed about with so great a cloud of witnesses, let us lay aside every weight, and the sin which doth so easily beset us, and let us run with patience the race that is set before us."

*Romans 8: 38-39*
"For I am persuaded, that neither death, nor life, nor angels, nor principalities, nor powers, nor things present, nor things to come, 39. Nor height, nor depth, nor any other creature, shall be able to separate us from the love of God, which is in Christ Jesus or Lord."

# Grace Got It

Many times on this Christian journey it is easy to get discouraged and back slide into what seems to be the easier life. We are reminded that the righteous will suffer many afflictions but the Lord will deliver us from them all.

When times get tough, God gets tougher. When the heat is turned up, God, the fourth man, is turned on. When people put on the pressure, God presses the release button. Please understand that the Will of God will never take you where the GRACE of GOD can't keep you. He gives us Amazing Grace for this Amazing Race!

*2 Corinthians 12:9*
"And he said unto me, My Grace is sufficient for thee: for my strength is made perfect in weakness. Most gladly therefore will I rather glory in my infirmities that the power of Christ may rest upon me."

**H**old To Heaven While Catching Hell

This is a cliché that many people often recite about the status of their lives: "Man, I am catching hell!" Hell refers to the trials, tribulations, and hardships that we frequently face. However, God reminded me that yes, you might be going through it but I am with you while you are fighting the fiery darts. We must keep our hands in his hands no matter what. One part of us wants to quit because we are catching hell, but the other part must stay connected to Heaven and keep fighting. If we hold on to Heaven long enough, God will eventually pull us up a little higher and take us out the fiery furnace. Letting go of God's hands is very dangerous and prohibits us from experiencing Heaven on Earth.

*Isaiah 41:13-14*
"For I the Lord thy God will hold thy right hand, saying unto thee, Fear not; I will help thee. *14.* Fear not, thou worm Jacob, and ye men of Israel; I will help thee, saith the Lord, and thy redeemer, the Holy One of Israel."

# Issue Is You

My life really didn't take flight until my Bishop told me these words, "Daughter, YOU are your own hold up! You have the gifts and power inside of you to conquer everything that confronts you!"

After he told me that, I jumped into turbo boost. I realized that I was my own hold up! If I was not successful, it was nobody's fault but mine. My success, my future, and my dreams were all up to me! The woman in the bible had an issue of blood for twelve long years, but when she touched Jesus she was made whole. You might not have an issue of blood but an issue of boldness. I dare you to examine yourself and birth out the boldness that God has planted in you.

*2 Corinthians 13:5*
"Test yourselves to see if you are in the faith; examine yourselves!" Or do you not recognize this about yourselves, that Jesus Christ is in you-unless indeed you fail the test?"

# NOTES

# Just In Time

If you look around, you'll see that we live in a microwave world. Many of us want things right now. As my dad would say, we want it fast, quick and in a hurry. Unfortunately, God does not operate like a microwave. God's blessings come to us "Just in Time!" God, our creator, knows what we need and when we need it. We can't get in a hurry and demand God to move on our "By Now Demands." For example, many of us find ourselves saying: I should have been married By Now. I should have had children By Now. I should have graduated By Now. In the lyrics of the gospel great, Dottie Peoples "He's an on time God. Yes, he is. He may not come when you want him, but He'll be there right on time!"

*Ecclesiastes 8:6*
"For there is a time and a way for everything, although man's trouble lies heavy on him.

*Isaiah 40:31*
"But they who wait for the Lord shall renew their strength; they shall mount up with wings like eagles; they shall run and not be weary; they shall walk and not faint. "

# Kindness is the Key

We have all heard the cliché "Kill them with Kindness." In Proverbs 18, the bible reminds us that "Man, should always show himself friendly." Basically, no matter how mad someone has made you, no matter how bad your day has been; Kindness is the Key! It's easy to frown during times of frustration. Let's face it; life can be hard at times. However, being kind in the midst of chaos, betrayal, loneliness, and tribulation gives God a chance to smile on you. Our father God loves it when His children can show kindness consistently.

We must give when we are grieved; Love when we are lonely, and Help others even when we are hurt.

*Proverbs 18: 24*
"A man *that hath* friends must shew himself friendly: and there is a friend *that* sticketh closer than a brother.

# L earn the Word

I believe that we will all be students until the day we die. We should learn something each and every day! The best book to study is the BIBLE. In order to pass the tests in life, we must study the word of God. I have learned that the answers to all of life's tests are written in God's Holy Word.
Many Christians find themselves quoting what their pastors say. Truly, there is nothing wrong

with that, but it wouldn't hurt to open the Bible for yourself and learn and read scripture in context.

*2 Timothy 2:15*
"Study to shew thyself approved unto God, a workman that needeth not to be ashamed, rightly dividing the word of truth."

*NOTES*

_____
_____
_____
_____
_____
_____
_____
_____

_____

_____

_____

_____

_____

_____

_____

_____

_____

_____

_____

_____

# Miraculous Madness

Sometimes you have to get fed up of being sick and tired and get just get Mad for your blessing. I'm reminded of the woman with the issue of blood for twelve long years. She suffered from this blood disease for twelve long years. No one and nothing could help her.  She heard that Jesus was coming by and she pressed her way to touch him. I can imagine she had a sense of drive and determination like never before. I can visualize her aggressiveness and "now or never" look on her face. She got MAD and MADE it happen.

Sometimes we have to get MAD and PRESS for our Miracle. You know that enough is enough and it's time for a healing, change, or reward.  I dare you to just get MAD and reach for your Miracle.

*Mark 5:25-34*

"A large crowd followed and pressed around Him. And a woman was there who had been subject to bleeding for twelve years. She had suffered a great deal under the care of many doctors and had spent all she had, yet instead of getting better she grew worse. When she heard about Jesus, she came up behind Him in the crowd and touched his cloak, because she thought, 'If I just touch His clothes, I will be healed.' Immediately her bleeding stopped and she felt in her body that she was freed from her suffering. At once Jesus realized that power had gone out from Him. He turned around in the crowd and asked, 'Who touched my clothes?' 'You see the people crowding against you,' His disciples answered, 'and yet you can ask, "Who touched Me?"' But Jesus kept looking around to see who had done it. Then the woman, knowing what had happened to her, came and knelt at His feet, and trembling with fear, told Him the whole truth. He said to her, 'Daughter, your faith has healed you. Go in peace and be freed from your suffering'"

# Never Say Never

We should never find ourselves in a place where we think we got it all together and are too good to make a mistake. Life has a way of knocking us down, turning us around, and putting us in our place. We strive for greatness, but every now and then, sin steps in. We should never say what we would never do. We pray to always do right and live right, but sometimes it gets a little hectic and wrong works better and feels better. Yes, your status in life requires you to be of good character: Pastor, Teacher, Mother, Entrepreneur. However, we should be mindful that at the end of the day, we are still human. Never Say Never-Always ask for Forgiveness.

*Romans 3:23*
For we all have sinned and come short of the glory of God.

# Obstacles are Ordered, Too

*Psalm 37:23* reminds us that "the steps of a good man are ordered by the Lord and he delights in his way." Even though your steps might be ordered, obstacles are placed along the way. As a result, we might trip or even fall but thanks be to God verse *24* says, "Though he falls, he shall not be utterly cast down; for the Lord upholdeth him with his hand." We must understand that along life's journey, stumbling blocks are needed. Some are there to make us Stop, Think, and Listen. Other obstacles are ordered to make us change our entire path. Whatever your obstacle has been—divorce, job loss, abuse, drug addiction, and/or sickness— just know that it was ordered to take you higher.

# Purpose in Pain

Make your pain work for you! We must understand that there is purpose for our pain. God allowed the affliction for a reason. It is our task to complete the assignment. David clearly admits that before he suffered pain; he was a problem child. It's clear that some of us have to hit rock bottom before we yield to Jesus. It is the pain that makes you forgive people, love people, and even be humble. Many of us are still going astray because we have not suffered enough.

*Psalm 119:67 (David)*
"Before I was afflicted I went astray, but now I obey your word."

# Quiet in the Storm

So many times we find ourselves trying to be God. We try to be God in our lives, our family lives, and our friends' lives. But clearly he says that "I am God." When storms are raging, we have to be still and let the winds blow and know that Jesus is the Captain of our Souls. The scripture says, "Rain falls on the just and the unjust." Even when you have faith, you'll still have difficulties, but when the storms come, you will not be defeated.

*Psalm 46:10*
"Be still and know that I am God!"

# Resist the Devil

It's really simple.  Stay away from the devil. We must not tarry in unclean places. We must avoid messy people. Resist means to walk away, ignore, and disconnect. By avoiding the devil, we allow ourselves room to submit to God. We have to come to a place in our lives when we no longer entertain foolishness but rather spotlight sacredness.

*James 4:7*
"Submit yourselves, then, to God. Resist the devil, and he will flee from you. ... So, humble yourselves before God. Resist the devil, and he will flee from you. [...]"

# Step Aside

When you face situations that seem impossible in your everyday life, God says, "I dare you to pray and ask me for it." The song-writer says, "Jesus can work it out-IF you let him!"

*Psalm 107:28-30*
"Then they cried to the LORD in their trouble, and he delivered them from their distress. He made the storm be still, and the waves of the sea were hushed. Then they were glad that the waters were

quiet, and he brought them to their desired haven."

# T otal Praise

We often here this cliché in church: "When the praises go up; the blessings come down!" I am a living witness because when I realized that my power came from praise, I was not afraid to shout and dance in church. Every time I lifted my hands, stomped my feet, and shouted Hallelujah, God had a blessing for me. We must give God our all.

*Psalm 27: 6*

"Therefore will I offer in his tabernacle sacrifices of joy; I will sing yea, I will sing praises unto the Lord."

# Unwavering Faith

Don't be pitiful when you can be powerful. Every day of your life has already been written in God's book and your story ends in victory. If you will get over what you think is a disadvantage, God will take what looks like a liability and turn it into an asset. God meets us at the level of our faith. Ordinary prayer gets ordinary results. Extraordinary prayer gets extraordinary results.

*Matthew 21:21*
"And Jesus answered and said to them, "Truly I say to you, if you have faith and do not doubt, you will not only do what was done to the fig tree, but even if you say to this mountain, 'Be taken up and cast away into the sea' it will happen."

# Vengeance is the Lord's but the Victory is Yours

God knew there'd be unfair situations. That's why He's already arranged a comeback for every setback, vindication for every wrong, a new beginning for every disappointment. When you walk in God's favor, honoring Him with your life, knowing who you are and Whose you are, you cannot be defeated.

*Psalm 41*
"The favor of God keeps my enemies from defeating me."

# What If?

What If God still says No to you in the new year? What If your dreams still don't come true in 2015? What If your Promise does not come to Pass? The answer is *Psalm 27:14,* "Wait on the Lord; be of good courage, and He shall strengthen thine heart: wait, I say, on the Lord."

So, if there is a **What if?** You just have to wait. **REMEMBER**—God loves you too much to open wrong doors. He's not letting you down; He's doing you a favor.

# AnXiety must eXit

Don't go around worried, nervous, anxious, and intimidated. The Creator of the universe has you in the palm of His hand. I know as humans, it is natural to worry. However, think on it for a little while and release it.

*Philippians 4:6-7*
"Be anxious for nothing, but in everything by prayer and supplication with thanksgiving let your requests be made known to God."
7. "And the peace of God, which surpasses all comprehension, will guard your hearts and your minds in Christ Jesus."

# Yes I Can

People will try to label you not good enough, too slow, too old, too many mistakes. You can't stop negative comments or prevent negative labels, but you can choose to not let them hold you back. You are equipped, anointed, strong and well able to do everything God has called you to do.

*Philippians 4:13*
"I can do all things through Christ who strengthens me."

# **Z**ip Your Lips

God has promised that if you'll turn matters over to Him and let Him handle them His way, He'll make your wrongs right. The title of my second single is "Hush." The lyrics to the song remind us to don't say one word because God hears our hearts and he feels our pain. We don't need to run and tell that or talk to a close friend when all we need to do is tell JESUS. Unfortunately, your best friend has a best friend too and your business can quickly spread like wild fires.

*Exodus 14:14*
"The Lord will fight for you while you keep silent."

My message to you:

Thanks for purchasing my first book. Please understand that as long as you live, you are going to have problems. As long as you wake up, you are going to face trials, tribulations, disappointments, confusions, and misunderstandings.

I pray that this book helps you to FOCUS. I also pray that you find the messages and scriptures to be a light in the dark places in your life. The Lord never promised us that this life would be easy, but he did promise to never leave us.

# ABOUT THE AUTHOR

LaToya Crawford is a sixth-grade Language Arts teacher in Quitman, Georgia. She loves to write, and she loves to inspire her students through writing. LaToya has taught reading and language arts for eleven years and has received numerous awards and recognition for her passion displayed for her pupils. In 2013, the Junior Leadership Council named her as a top teacher and mentor in the nation. In 2004, she was a Disney Teacher of the Year nominee.

Although education is her daily duty, LaToya is also a television personality, recording artist, and minister. She was introduced to the world in 2000 when she became a television news reporter for WCTV Eyewitness News in Tallahassee, Florida. After two years of chasing criminals and beating deadlines, she decided to trade the camera for the classroom.

Even though LaToya loves teaching kids, she still longed to make an impact on the big screen. In the summer of 2013, she started her own television show on the cable channel in her hometown of Thomasville, Georgia. The show is entitled, "A Moment of Inspiration." The show is designed to empower, inspire, and motivate viewers by highlighting the struggles and victories of others.

Many people witness LaToya's passion and charisma in the classroom and on television, but her power really shines in the pulpit. LaToya became an ordained evangelist nearly four years ago, and she has blessed congregations all over the world with her life changing and soul saving sermons.

In addition to preaching the gospel, she sings about the goodness of God as well. She became a renowned gospel-recording artist in 2013 and made her national television debut on Dr. Bobby Jones Gospel in May of 2013. She performed her hit single, "HUSH."

At the end of the day, LaToya embraces her seven-year-old son, Andre Williams, Jr. He has many gifts and has a bright future ahead of him.

LaToya travels around the country singing, preaching, and teaching to God's people. You can follow her on Facebook or You tube. You can also book LaToya for your next conference, revival, or gospel explosion (229) 403-4813. Also visit her website: www.blessings12.wix.com/latoyacrawford.

Made in the USA
Columbia, SC
01 April 2021